HOW TO KILL YOUR GIRLFRIEND'S CAT again

HOW TO KILL YOUR GIRLFRIEND'S CAT again

♦♦♦♦♦♦♦♦♦♦♦♦♦♦♦♦♦♦♦♦♦♦♦♦♦♦♦♦♦♦♦

Dr. Robert Daphne

with illustrations by

Susan Davis

St. Martin's Press · New York

Library of Congress Cataloging-in-Publication Data

Daphne, Robert.
    How to kill your girlfriend's cat again / by Robert Daphne.
      p. cm.
    ISBN 0-312-05100-X
    1. Cats—Humor. I. Title.
PN6162.D347   1990
818'.5402—dc20   90-37323
                                           CIP

First Edition: November 1990
10 9 8 7 6 5 4 3 2 1

For Louis:
The Thing That Wouldn't Die.

Introduction

You can't believe it. She got another cat. After months of plotting you rid yourself of the first one, the hideous Louis. She never suspected. It was your finest moment. You followed the step-by-step directions in *How to Kill Your Girlfriend's Cat.* Perhaps you chose the quicksand kitty litter technique. Louis crept into his box and sank out of your life forever. Perhaps you bought the electric scratchpost, flicked the hidden switch when your girlfriend left the house, and Louis reached up to play, receiving enough electricity to charge Philadelphia for two years.

Or maybe you invited wrestlers over to "play with the cat"? Or bred the twenty-two foot mouse? Or called the secret number to hire the cat hit men from Minneapolis? Three nights later, the kitchen hutch "accidentally fell" on Louis.

Whichever method you chose, the demon was gone, gloriously removed from your life forever. Oh joyous joy! You threw a party and your friends actually came, because there was no cat to be allergic to anymore. Your third couch in a month *still looked new four hours later!* You stopped waking from drowning nightmares at 3:00 A.M. to find Louis sitting on your face. You no longer had to arrange napalm runs with the Pentagon to deodorize the hall.

So many happy memories of freedom. The pharmacist lost his condo without your business. You didn't need so much iodine for scratch marks any more. Your boss stopped eyeing the streaks on your forearms and administering drug tests. A whole month went by without your having to use the Heimlich maneuver on a dinner guest choking on a furball.

But just when you thought it was safe to go back into the living room, it's Louis II! You can hear your girlfriend even as you read this, cooing to him, "Are you my one? (kiss) I love you (kiss). Are you my little cat, my darling buddy woo?"

Sure you're grinding your teeth. Who wouldn't be? You were terrific, the way you carried out that first catricide. You controlled yourself beforehand. You petted him for weeks before you killed him, to fool your girlfriend into thinking you liked him. You rushed home from fun nights out because "Louis might be lonely." You bought him kitty treats and fed them to him by hand, while you scratched him behind the ears. You fooled her, all right. You fooled her so well she bought another one. She even gave it the same name. Louis.

First, let's get over the recriminations. Maybe you overdid the sobbing when the monster was buried. Maybe you shouldn't have used the whole bottle of theatrical tears. Or perhaps you should have gotten her a replacement pet. A cocker spaniel. Or even a gila monster. Anything but a cat.

But now that you're ready to think again, let's not waste time over spilt milk. You still love the girl, don't you? Isn't a lifetime of bliss worth one more itty-bitty murder? Not even a murder really. After all, is stepping on a cockroach murder? Or curing a plague? The good news is, since the original *How to Kill Your Girlfriend's Cat* was published, Harvard researchers have made new breakthroughs in revenge planning. New techniques that even experts thought were accidents were unearthed in Sumer, where cats were once *really* hated.

How to Kill Your Girlfriend's Cat Again will list tried and true methods used by masters through the ages, including Edgar Allan Poe, Beethoven, Charles Manson, and even a former President of the United States, who managed to come up with a way to murder the First Lady's cat with the press watching, and no one ever suspected the truth!

These techniques are guaranteed to provide the relief you desperately crave, dispatching the odious feline, no matter how many lives it has, to the great litterbox in the sky.

A word of caution. Cats are clever, and far more insidious than most people think. Over the centuries, hated by all decent forms of life, they have evolved a highly sensitive radar for detecting when a plot is afoot. *How to Kill Your Girlfriend's Cat Again* will instruct you on how to avoid the pitfalls of feline destruction, and how to keep the wretched animal from turning the tables on you. Don't forget that Cleopatra's cat, "Pharoah," engineered the assassination of Julius Caesar, and Marie Antoinette's "Chuckles" caused the beheading of the entire royal family of France.

But you are smarter than a mere animal, aren't you? Don't you remember how wonderful life was when no cat lived in your house? When your landlord would refund your entire damage deposit when you moved, and not keep it to "clean up after Hermes"? She's worth fighting for, isn't she? As that great cat hater Aesop said, "If at first you don't succeed, try, try again."

But you'll have to be sly this time. Henry the Eighth, who successfully rid himself of his wives' forty-seven cats, said, "You have to be more subtle after the first one, or she'll figure it out."

Relief is at hand. With Louis out of your life, love will triumph. This time you'll do it right, and nothing will get in the way of your glorious future.

HOW TO KILL YOUR GIRLFRIEND'S CAT again

The Mexican Cat Dance

It comes from those sunny lands south of the border. The "Pancho Villa Five," a mariachi band, can be rented. When they crash through the door, trumpets blaring, announce to your girlfriend, "Why go to a restaurant and share these guys with other diners? For you, my love, money is no object." When the band starts stomping the cat, and your girlfriend becomes nervous, laugh and say, "It's only an act." When the band leaves, shake the flattened torso of Louis that is sticking to the dining room floor, and try to wake him, angrily saying, "Hey! They were serious!"

Rawhide Collar

This attractive replica of the Old West brings to mind the words of Davy Crockett, who said, "When men were men and cats were cats, and never the twain should meet." Invented by frontiersmen to rid themselves of these colonial pests, the rawhide collar comes in a pack that says "flea collar." As you buckle the soft leather strap around the hated Louis's neck, pet him lovingly and tell your girlfriend, "That other collar looked like it hurt." Make sure the rawhide collar is moist when you tie it on, because as it dries it shrinks. Two hours later, when you find Louis in the closet, proclaim, "This is defective! I'm going to sue!"

Kitty Litter

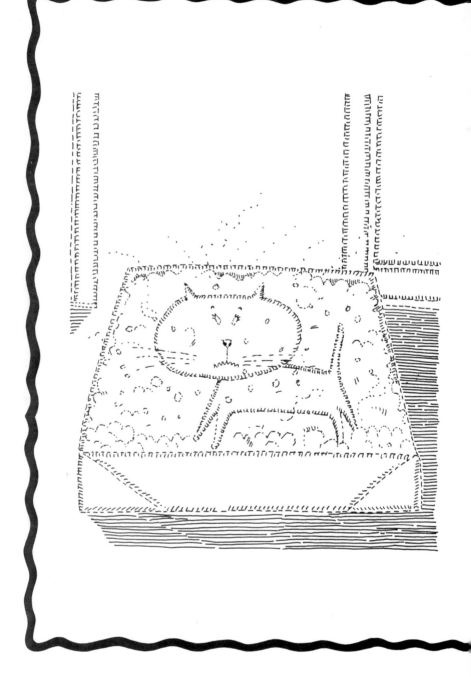

Asbestos-Lined Cat Box

Looks like a regular cat box, in attractive pale colors like pink and blue. Fill it with kitty litter, stand back, and wait. The instant the cat enters the box, proven carthenogenic substances will swing into action. Asbestos is guaranteed to clog lungs and other vital organs. Before you can say, "Here, kitty, kitty," Louis will emerge, tottering, and after three more trips will be dispatched to that great litterbox in the sky. If you have an aversion to asbestos, radon can be substituted.

Samurai Declawing Technique

If you think cats do damage in America, imagine ancient Japan, where houses were made of paper, and four-hundred-year-old prize bonsai trees were the size of scratching posts? The samurai class rose as a whole to get rid of cats. Today, call a rent-a-samurai, and your relationship with Louis will improve after he's been declawed.

Wondro Glue! You Can Do Craaaaazy Things with It!

A simple dab on the feline's back, and the term "male bonding" takes on new meaning. This new miracle fluid provides an excellent means for curing the sticky problem. Your cat will form instant attachments that will draw it away from your house.

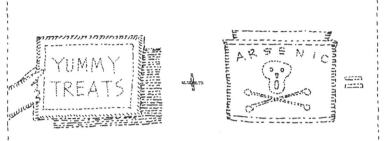

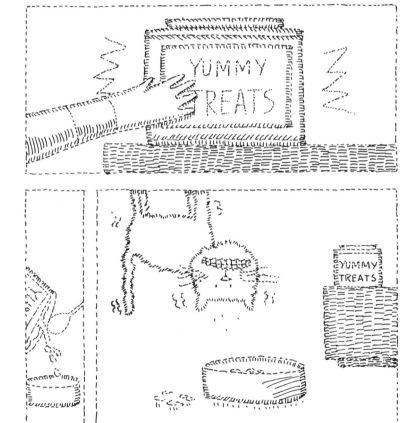

Fake Labels

Easy and cheap. These brightly colored, attractive fake labels, available at any kill-your-cat shop, fit perfectly over cans of arsenic, rat poison, and a host of common household items. Lick the back of the label and affix it to any posion. Voilà! The toilet bowl cleaner now says, "Yummy, delicious kitty treats!" When convulsions begin, pooh-pooh them away. "Just another furball, honey."

The Great Italian Tenor, Pavarotti, Shatters Glass

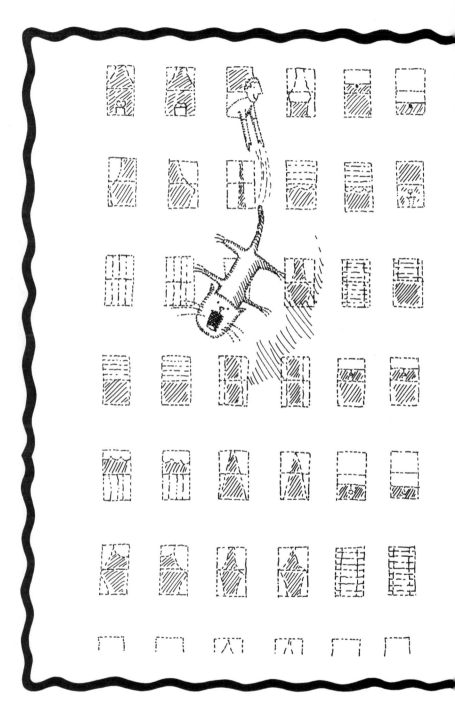

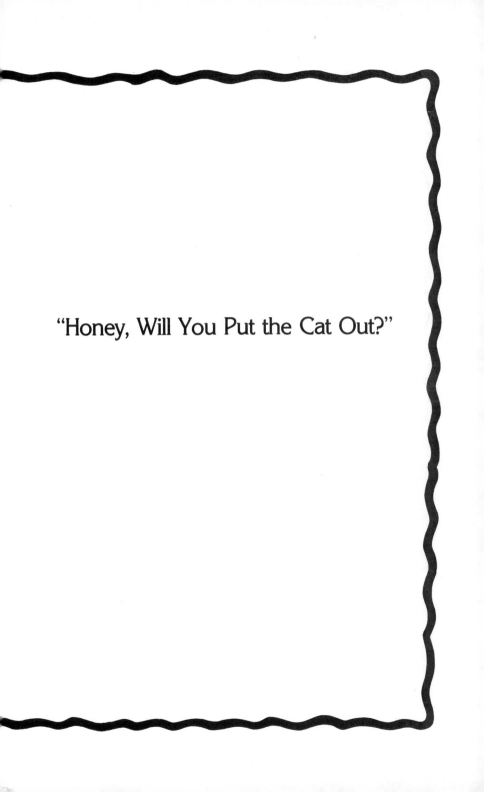

"Honey, Will You Put the Cat Out?"

Star Wars Food Dish

Developed by a former President of the United States to get rid of his wife's cat. The beauty of the star wars food dish, which resembles a regular food dish, is that you can get rid of the cat without ever going near it. You know that Louis roams the neighborhood bothering everyone, so you place the dish in an empty lot down the block. Fill the dish with Louis's favorite food, disgusting old tuna or rotted intestines. The instant the horrible little snout touches the dish, sensors inside the plastic trigger killer satellites deep in outer space. A laser beam flashes from the sky like a bolt of justice. It will all be over before you can say "cinders."

Dr. Mengele's Boarding Facility

Going on a trip? Tell your girlfriend, "We can't leave poor Louis alone! Suppose he knocks over the food dish and starves!" Dr. Mengele's Boarding Home, which until recently was operated only in Paraguay, has now opened branches in most North American cities. When you return home, the distraught "doctor" will present you with a full report of how "Ze cat caught un cold in ze shower."

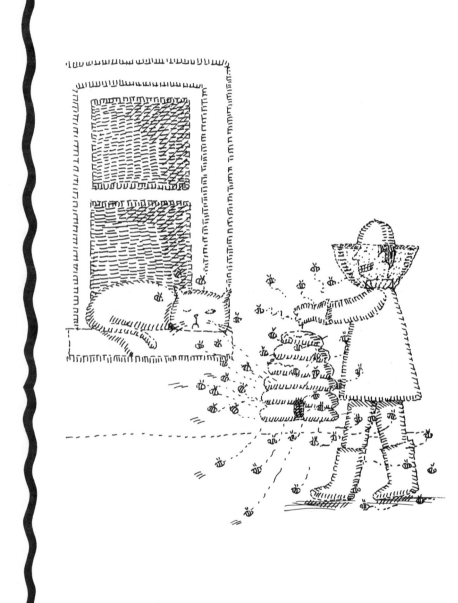

Killer Bees Strike in New Jersey!
(Reprinted from the New York Post*)*

We've known for years that they're coming! Trenton, New Jersey, was attacked Tuesday night by a swarm of dreaded South American killer bees! The bees flew into one home, where they attacked a pet cat named Louis, stinging him mercilessly. Louis had been lounging by the sill and must have just eaten pollen, because the substance coated his body. Jersey residents are urged to be on the lookout for the swarm, which disappeared after the attack. Princeton scientists are wondering why no attacks have occurred between New Jersey and northern Mexico, where the swarm was last sighted.

The Charles Manson Technique

This is a good method for boyfriends who want to get rid of old furniture and a girlfriend's cat at the same time. Wait until your girlfriend is going out, and tell her that you are going out of town. She thinks you're in Cincinnati visiting your mother. When she comes back to the apartment all the furniture is smashed, and someone has spray-painted "Acid is groovy" and "Kill the Pigs" all over the walls. The press loves satanic cult stories. The police will never suspect you.

Auntie Junie's Baby

If you think average babies are hard on pets, you've never seen Auntie Junie's baby in action. Actually a tiny Bulgarian midget, Auntie Junie's baby was trained by the KGB and the great behavioral scientist Pavlov to have an unprecedented hatred of cats. His tiny fists have been strengthened to squeeze, his cute milk teeth to bite like a tiger. Contact Auntie Junie. You can "hire her" as a maid, cook, or babysitter. She shows up with her cute baby, Kronkovitch (a former weightlifter for the Moscow circus). When you return not only will the house be spotless, but Auntie Junie will be beside herself. "The little cat," she will moan, over and over, "The poor little cat...."

Ways That Went Wrong

Never underestimate the enemy. Cats are insidious. They always remember a slight and strike back, often with disastrous results. In order to help you avoid problems, here are three historic examples when the beasts turned the tables.

Distemper Shot

The Good St. Catrick, Patron Saint of Boyfriends

Substitute Dead Cat Order Form

One obstacle that has puzzled cat killers for years is how to rid themselves of the animal and still avoid signs of violence upon the body. The problem is solved! Simply fill out the substitute dead cat form, available at any kill-your-cat shop. Make sure to describe the monster perfectly, down to the disgusting amoeba-shaped white spot on his nose, the exact length of its detestable shedding tail, and the murderous blue of his eyes. Mail the form and wait. Three days later a plain brown package will arrive labeled FREE SAMPLE. Inside you will find a cat, dead of natural causes, a perfect replica of Louis! Now you can indulge your most sadistic fantasies upon the real thing. Feed Louis to the killer whales. Throw a hand grenade into his food bowl. Run him over with bulldozers. The body your girlfriend sees, dead from peaceful causes, will be the one that came in the mail.

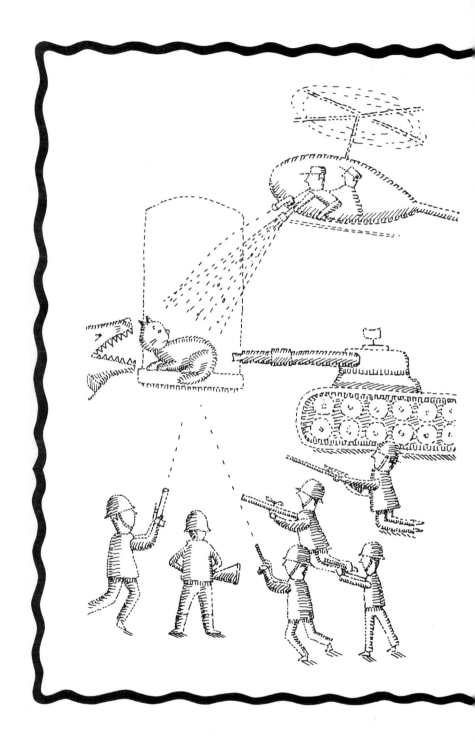

Make This Phonecall to Your Police *Swat* Squad Emergency Number

"Hello, it's... get away from me! It's rabid! Eeeeeaaaaa-ggghhh! No, no, don't bite me again! I'm at Twenty-one Hampton street... trapped by... the cat, it's... WON'T SOMEBODY SAAAAAAVE MEEEEE?!" Click.

What Do You Mean You Lost Our Luggage? Louis Was in That Case!

The "airport mixup" technique, commonly used by frequent travelers, can be accomplished with a simple sleight-of-hand trick. While the ticket agent is occupied, palm a bunch of airport labels. Favorites include Managua, Beirut, and Kabul. The "airline mixup" will result in Louis winging his way to any one of several vicious battle zones around the world.

How Beethoven Killed His Girlfriend's Cat

Beethoven was a maestro in more ways than one. The old trail of food method and a grand piano were all he needed for success! Louis's demise accounts for the terrific crashing noise in the master's Eighth Symphony.

ENTERTAINMENT
CENTER

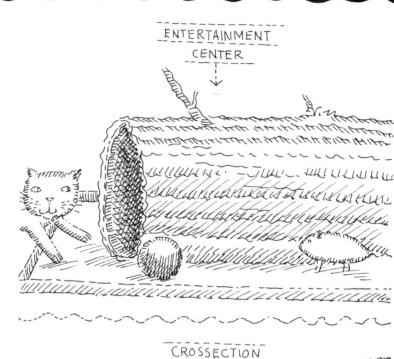

CROSSECTION

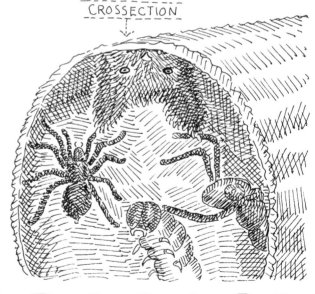

Cat Entertainment Center

Aren't you the perfect boyfriend? You bought Louis a present. Cats check in, but they don't check out. Looks like a regular play center, with cute passageways the cat can explore inside an old log. Louis creeps right in. Twenty minutes later, when he's still inside, your girlfriend becomes worried. Tell her, "Oh, honey, he came out ten minutes ago when you were in the other room." When Louis doesn't come back from "outside," put up reward signs all over the neighborhood. What do you have to worry about? You're free, free!

Toxic Gas Carpet Deodorizer

Originally used by Otto von Bismark in the First World War to rid British trenches of unpleasant odors, this handy household item not only eliminates kitty odors, but their root causes as well. The efforts last only twenty minutes and leave your house smelling as fresh as the Mediterranean, a mountain stream, or an Alpine meadow, depending on which scent you choose. Set the can in the middle of the room. Go out for a half hour. Although Louis will be inert when you return, medical authorities will say "heart attack."

Play Parlor Games with Louis

Hours of fun! Guests may want to participate too. The more the merrier when it comes to these action games!

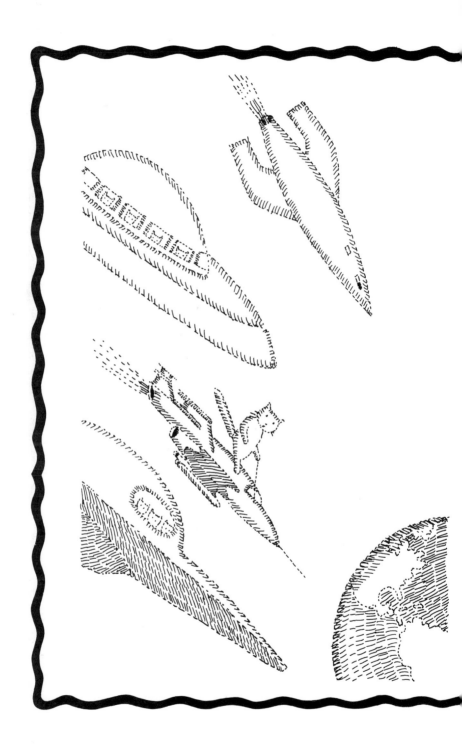

Where Aliens Go to Get Rid of
Girlfriends' Cats

Feed the Cat a Giant Furball

Start an Ugly Rumor

What's Wrong with Suspended Animation?

Your girlfriend has come home from work to discover that you've put Louis in the freezer. It is true that the situation looks grim for you at first. There he lies, like the monster in *The Thing,* unblinking, unmoving, un-anything. "I did it to save him!" you cry. "He was getting old! I couldn't bear watching him lose strength this way! Now we can keep him until science invents a way to increase his life span. He's not dead, darling. He's only sleeping!"

After a while, your girlfriend will see that your concern for Louis was prompted by love. You can even open the freezer while you eat dinner, so the three of you can be together regularly. Throw out the science pages of the paper, though, in case someone really discovers how to wake Louis from suspended animation.

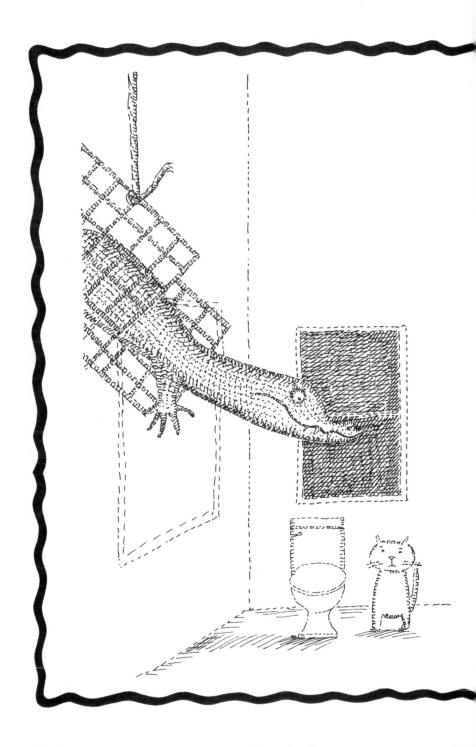

Giant Alligator Climbs Out of New York Toilet!

(Reprinted from the National Screamer*)*

In a horrible and puzzling incident, police rushed to a Manhattan high rise last week to find a ten-foot alligator thrashing around in a bathroom high above the ground! Fortunately, the couple who lived in the apartment were out at the time, and the only victim of the reptile's hunger was a pet cat, Louis. "Lots of people used to flush baby alligators down the toilet," said a police spokesman. "It must have lived down in the sewers for years, growing larger every day. But I can't figure out how it squeezed through the little toilet opening. Oh, well. Too bad we can't ask the alligator."

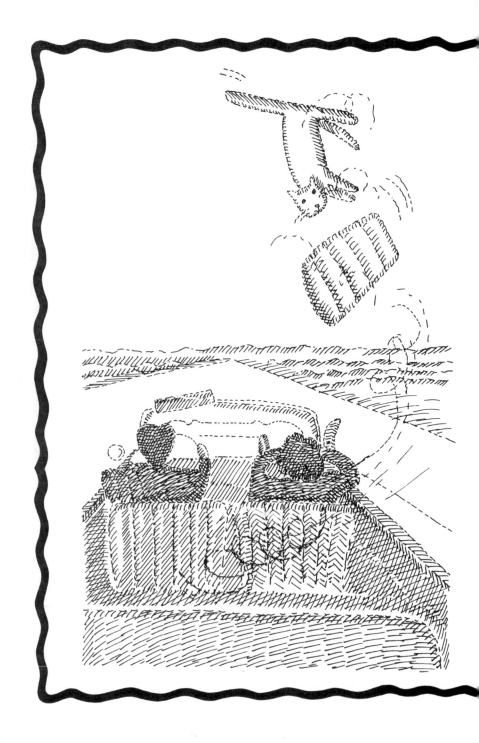

Jack-in-the-Box Car Cushion

For those fun Sunday drives in the country.

Help Those Less Fortunate Than Yourselves

Medical studies have shown that pets have a calming effect on violent people. One Saturday, put down the paper, squeeze your girlfriend and say, "Honey, we're blessed with each other, and we should share our happiness with those more needy than ourselves." Take the cat to the penitentiary and insist that Louis visit "The Morningside Heights Strangler" in the maximum security wing. When the hour visit is up, and the warden brings out the limp Louis in his arms, angrily exclaim, "I'm sick of these liberal prison programs. I'm glad I voted for George Bush!"

The Chimney Kitty Vacuum Attachment

Louis has heard a strange noise in the chimney and steps inside to investigate. The instant he steps on the hidden switch, the giant cat vacuum attachment, which you bought at your kill-the-cat shop, switches on. A powerful draft of air sweeps the hapless Louis into the puncture-proof dustbag. Later, your girlfriend may report that she hears muffled animal cries from inside the chimney. "Darn," you say. "Birds! Tomorrow I'll clean them out."

Alfred Hitchcock's *"Gaslight"* Technique

A subtle means, used by Charles Boyer against Ingrid Bergman in the film *Gaslight*. Originally, this was supposed to be a movie about killing cats, but kitty lovers forced Hollywood to change it.

If you opt for the *Gaslight* technique, convince your girlfriend she is going mad. Plant tape recorders around the house. When the recorders switch on at varying times of the day or night, emitting horrible screams and meows, tell your girlfriend, "*I* didn't hear anything." In the middle of dinner suddenly say, "Don't talk that way about Louis! I thought you liked him!" When your girlfriend says she didn't say anything to start with, cock your head and say, "Honey, are you okay?" Shoot off guns at 3:00 A.M. and then pretend to be asleep. Demand, "Why are you looking at Louis so horribly?"

When your girlfriend's mental state has sufficiently deteriorated, eliminate the cat any way you choose, carry the corpse into the bedroom, weeping, and scream, "Sadist! He was just an animal!" The psychiatrist will agree that she had hidden aggressions against Louis.

More Ways That Went Wrong:
George Armstrong Custer

How the Great King Nebuchadnezzar Got the Idea for Babylon's Famous "Hanging Gardens"

BEFORE

AFTER

Machiavelli's Disguise Kit

Machiavelli, who never did anything directly, got rid of his girlfriend's first cat, but then had to cope with another. This Italian genius is credited with inventing the disguise kit, still sold in kill-your-cat shops everywhere. Use the kit before the cat goes out. Extend the whiskers. Change the color of the fur with the special waterproof dye. Small contact lenses will give Louis's eyes a yellow, puss-ridden color. And the coup de grace is the stuffed rat you glue to Louis's mouth. Hours later when Louis comes home, not only will your girlfriend not recognize him, she'll scream, "Get that animal away from here! It keeps trying to get in the house." As much as you hate to call the humane society, you will do it, and Louis will be gone forever.

How Rube Goldberg Killed His Girlfriend's Cat

Try a Recombinant DNA
Experiment to Turn the Cat into a
Friendlier Animal

Killing Cats Has Spurred Many Discoveries Through the Ages

(From the Kill-Your-Cat Archives in Washington, D.C.)

Donate the Cat for Safety Research

Crash dummy tests.

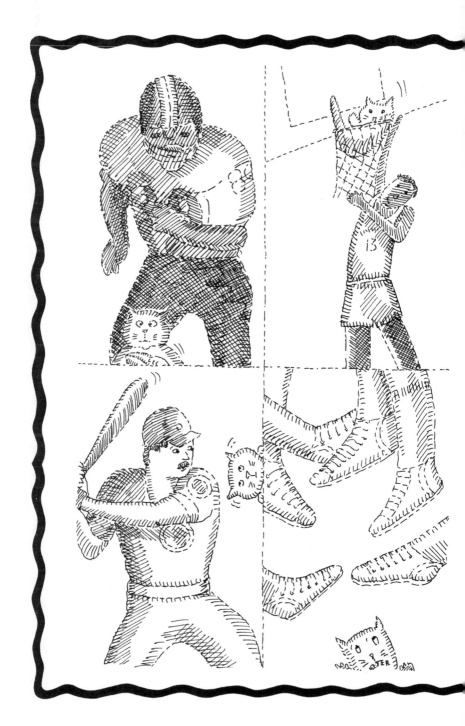

Teach the Cat Sports

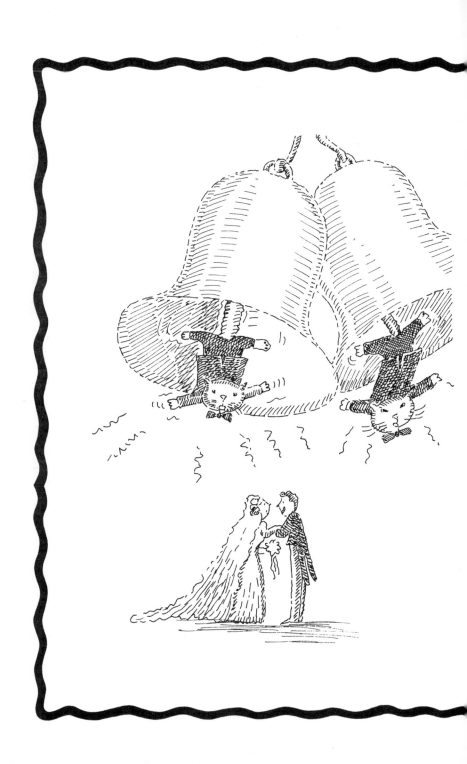

Postscript

Louis is gone now, and don't you feel terrific? However, your job is not over yet. You have to make sure you're not caught, and you have to be guaranteed your girlfriend doesn't get a *third* cat.

First, to protect yourself, throw out or burn any evidence, including this book. Or, if you can't bring yourself to get rid of the book, lend it to another suffering boyfriend, or slip on a phony cover like *The Book of Physics*. Wipe the little carcass of all fingerprints. Immediately join the National Wildlife Federation and the ASPCA to show your girlfriend how much you love animals. You might even participate in the adopt-a-manatee program in Florida. Don't worry. The manatee never comes to the house. These techniques will guarantee that if your girlfriend should begin to suspect the truth later on, she will dismiss it. And if one of her friends suggests you had anything to do with Louis's demise, she will never see that person again.

If, after employing these methods, you think she might still guess what happened, slip into a public phone booth and call her. Say, "The friends of Afghanistan take credit for our terrorist triumph. Louis was a Communist swine!"

Immediately move your residence and sign a new lease prohibiting cats, with torture as a penalty if you break the lease.

Whenever you pass a cat on the street, or visit a friend who has one, use the sneezing powder you bought at the kill-your-cat shop to establish your new "allergy." Phony doctors' notes can be easily drawn up. Any signature will do. The second your girlfriend accepts that you really have an allergy say, "Darn, and I was going to buy you another cat."

Finally, if the subject of Louis comes up, weep copiously, swoon on the floor, and say things like, "I can't go through it again!" Fake nightmares are good too. Wake your girlfriend in the middle of the night, sobbing. "It was another Louis dream. This time he was at the beach with us. He was so cute, so cute."

Grief will bring you together. These timeless techniques have rid boyfriend cat sufferers everywhere from the curse of the kitty. Thousands, if not millions, of happy relationships have prospered after initial cat problems were overcome. Congratulations. You've rid yourself of the creature. Now go out and celebrate. Throw out the kitty litter, the Nine Lives, and the kitty toys.

If your girlfriend insists on getting a third cat, stay tuned for the next volume, *How to Kill Your Girlfriend.*